A Wee Cromdale Loon

A Wee Cromdale Loon

JAMES MCQUEEN

Acknowledgments to: -

Friends:-
Jimmy McLean, Irene Galasso, Billy, and Barney Campbell.

My cousin, Helen McAdam, and my Daughter Dawn.

Thanks to Katie Dennis of Stevenage Photographic

'For fame and for fortune I wandered the earth and now I've come back to this land of my birth, I've brought back my treasures but only to find they're less than the pleasures I first left behind

For these are my mountains and this is my glen. The braes of my childhood will know me again. No lands ever claimed me, though far I did roam for these are my mountains I have come home!!!!'

Jimmie.

CONTENTS

1. JUST A WEE LOON

I have decided to call this book A Wee Loon from Cromdale, as that is exactly what I was.

Being a boy, I was a loon, but had I been born a girl, I would have been a quine. Loon and quine were part of the dialect of North East Scotland, the beautiful land where I was born, and this dialect was known as Broad Scots or Doric.

For example, 'Aye, ma loon, foo'r yie dooin the day?' (Hello, my boy, how are you today?) We were not allowed to use any of these words in the classroom, unfortunately, as we had to speak 'proper' English.

I have a few recollections as a very wee loon, such as the terrible snowstorm when I was about three, with the man with a big, red caterpillar tractor trying to clear the snow from outside the front of our house; and the time that I was late for Cromdale Public School when I was five. The teacher asked me where I'd been, so I told her that I'd been playing with a wee moosie that I found at the Mill Road end. Another recollection from around the same time was the one and only time my mother took me down to school, on my first day. I can still see her now, in her yellow headscarf with a black lining strip around it.

My mother, Anna, was a rather quiet and timid woman, but my grandmother, Granny McQueen, was the boss, the family matriarch, and she held the family together after my grandfather died. She wasn't a big woman, but she was big in spirit. We lived a mile up the hill from the village of Cromdale, in the East Lethendry Farmhouse. Also living there were my uncles, Peter and Donny, who worked on the farm. Peter looked after the sheep and cattle, and I remember getting up early and going out lambing ewes with him before I went to school. Donny did all the manual work; he was immensely strong, and when he was training to throw the hammer at the Highland games, I had to watch where it landed and drag it back so he could throw it again. As I grew older, he taught me to drive the tractor and do jobs like ploughing and harrowing. I used to follow close behind him when he went out with his 12-bore shotgun, to shoot rabbits, hares, pigeons, and the odd pheasant, 'for the pot'.

In the winter time on a Saturday morning, the threshing mill would be put on, driven by a big black engine. I would be up in the loft handing the sheaves of corn over to Uncle Peter, he would cut the string and feed them into the fast-revolving drum: a very noisy, dusty procedure. Donny would be down below, taking off the sacks of grain and stacking the straw further along the barn.

Uncle Sandy lived with us but worked on a neighbouring farm. My mother and grandmother ran the house, looking after the poultry and dealing with all the vans: bakers, fishermen, butchers, and grocers. I got on well with my uncles and my mum and grandmother, although my grandmother was an invalid for a long time. She had terrible varicose veins and health problems in her later years, but I still remember that there would always be a few dogs and cats following her when she went to milk the cows, waiting for a plate of milk.

East Lethendry Farm covered what had been a lot of small farms or crofts, their ruins still quite visible, as well as a lot of Scottish history, with the moors leading up to the Cromdale Hills where the Battle of Cromdale was fought in 1690. The large wood up on Cromdale Hill took its name from a nearby gulley called Corie na h-Eirigh, so over the years the pronunciation sounds more like this. 'Corna Herrie'. That is the name handed down by generations of McQueens, woodcutters, gamekeepers, poachers, and other local folk. The prominent cairn at the top of this hill was built to commemorate the crowning of King Edward VII and Queen Alexandra, back in 1902, although I didn't know the history at the time. At the top of Corna Herrie wood, down from the cairn, sticking out of the heather is the Piper's Stone, where a piper stood playing as the battle of Cromdale raged around him. Little did I know that in August 2001 I would stand on the stone and play 'The Haughs O' Cromdale' on my bagpipes, surrounded by a pipe band I had formed, the City of Bristol Pipes and Drums.

This area was the favourite hunting ground of my dog June and I. Together, we used to catch mountain hares for the pot at home, and I'd sell some of them to the old ladies in the village. For some reason, June did not have the long hair that collies usually have – hers was sleek and close – and she was extremely fast. She'd chase the hares and when they disappeared into their escape holes, I would run and block the exit, causing her to start barking and yelping with excitement.

We'd dig down through the soft, peaty soil, then I would pull them out and put them to sleep.

We lived near Cliff Cottage, which was about 500 yards down from East Lethendry, and to get to it you had to go down a slope and through a little bit of wood. Living there was Granny Bell; Jimmy McLean (father); Margie, his wife; their sons, Jimmy and Willie; and also Pat Bell, granddaughter of Granny Bell. Young Jimmy, five years older than me, was my idol. I followed him everywhere, being taught how to trap ferrets and snare rabbits. He taught me how to gut and skin them, and sometimes we'd build stones, light a fire, put a bit of old netting wire over the top, and cook the rabbits on it; just like a modern-day B.B.Q. Willie was three years older than me; we got up to lots of things together, like playing in the ruined Lethendry Castle and dooking (swimming), playing about with other loons in the River Spey and he had a great desire to climb very tall trees. One day he, a lad called Jim Fraser, and I dragged an old tin bath all the way across the moors to near a few houses called Burnside. We had previously found a little dam and thought we could paddle and play around in the bath. All was going fine until we saw two men coming up towards us – Mr. Connon, manager of the Balmenach Distillery, and wee Charlie Grant – so we threw all our clothes into the bath and took off as fast as we could across the moor, with them shouting after us. Apparently, we had been in the dam that was the domestic water supply for the worker's houses.

Pat Bell was a year younger than me; she was a bit of a tomboy and often came up to East Lethendry. Life was spent outdoors from dawn to dusk sledging in the snow and helping on the farm but if the weather was really bad, we could always go into the barn or byres with the animals.

When I was eleven, I was old enough to go to 'the beating' with Jim Anderson, the gamekeeper, who lived in the 'Keepers Hoose', down the brae from East Lethendry. Grouse shooting always started on the glorious 12th of August, and about 15–20 of us youngsters would assemble outside the Cromdale shop and be driven up a hillside somewhere in the area, where we were issued with a flag on the end of a stick. The gamekeepers would take us up the hill, dropping one off about every 50 yards, there'd be a blast on a whistle and off we'd go! We'd walk along the hillside, through some very deep heather, shouting and making the grouse fly out in front of us, for perhaps a mile. The 'toffs', as we called them, the wealthy people, would be in 'butts', trenches dug into the ground – and they'd start shooting the grouse as they flew overhead. We would repeat the 'drives' once again before having a packed lunch, then do another two 'drives' in the afternoon. It was a welcome bit of pocket money; the wage was 10/- per day – about 50p in today's money.

As well as beating for grouse I also made 10/- a day lifting tatties – the English word being potatoes. When I was about 12 and had started at Grantown School, I spent all of my October holidays with a gang of other youngsters, in potato fields at different farms in the area. There were sticks in the ground to indicate where each of us had to pick the tatties, and the digger would come along and churn them out for us. I usually found the first two days the worst on my back, but after that, it wasn't too bad. If I finished my stint quickly enough, the gentleman in me would rush down and help the girls finish theirs before the digger came around again!

Thinking back, I never really had a lot of parental guidance with regard to schooling. When I was at Cromdale School I was taken through my spelling, reading, and times tables, also poetry. I remember something about 'a host of golden daffodils' but at Grantown School, I would sit at the kitchen table at night and do whatever homework I had. Basically, I was keeping my head above water.

In hindsight, it was good that I was never forced down the academic route, being a white-collared worker, would not have suited me. Fortunately, at the age of 16, I was accepted into the Royal Marines – which is a story yet to come.

I went to Cromdale Public School, where Mr Baird was headmaster, ably assisted by Mrs Baird, from the age of five until I was 12. There were only five of us in the class: Helen Miller, my cousin; Margaret Baxter; Gordon Davidson; Barney Campbell; and myself. On prize-giving day Helen always got first prize, and I was usually behind in second place. I have only happy memories of Cromdale School.

Grantown School was a different kettle of fish! I think I was starting to grow up, finding my way, and I started talking back to teachers, then getting the belt (a thick leather strap with two thongs on it). You had to hold your hand out, up, and they whacked you.

I remember Mrs. McIntosh, who took us for arithmetic, I back-chatted her a few times. She used to send one of the girls through to another teacher who'd enquire, 'Who is it for this time!?' It was also unfortunate that sitting in that class was my young cousin Peter, five years my junior. I remember one night going back to his house and my auntie Margaret telling me sternly that she knew I'd been in trouble.

Another teacher who liked to keep us in line with the belt was Mr. Thornton, a history teacher and a great big man. He was in another world, away in the clouds as far as I was concerned, but he didn't shy away from doling out the punishments, even if the reasons were fairly ridiculous. I think he must have asked us what we did at the weekend on one occasion and I put my hand up – 'Yes boy, what?!' – and said I'd been beating for grouse for the Duke of Luxemburg. He poo-pooed me immediately. 'Don't be stupid, boy!' In his book, I'd obviously back-chatted him, so I got the belt! You had to lift your hand up high so your jacket or jersey moved up, and all the blood vessels on my wrist were red and blue. I was not over the moon about that.

Thornton, during his history lessons, taught us about battles the Scots fought against the English, but he never taught us about an important local battle!! The Battle of Cromdale took place at the Haughs of Cromdale on 30th April and 1st May 1690. Or about the Piper who played during it on the 'Pipers Stone'. Nearby Lethendry Castle, what was the significance of it?

He never taught us about The Battle of Culloden that took place on 16 April 1746 on Drummossie Moor near Inverness, 20+ miles away. Years later I would find out my Great times eight Grandfather Cpt. Hugh Cameron died there fighting for Bonnie Prince Charlie against the Government forces.

Another time I suffered from this article of torture was on the day that I was going to the Army Cadet party in Elgin and we were in the music room. Music for us wasn't playing instruments, it was always singing from books. Mrs Calder was the lady that normally took us, but she was off sick and a minister was put in charge, Reverend Hogg. He was a big fellow too! I was mucking about with a girl sitting beside me, Audrey Campbell, and he called me out to the front to make an example of me. Whack!! He gave me two of the worst and hardest hits I ever had! A Scottish minister! So that put me in my place.

Prefects, senior boys who were destined for great academic lives ahead of them, had the authority to give you a whack (s) on your buttocks if you committed misdemeanors. I locked horns with some of them. The only one I had any time for was Geordie McInnes from Carr Bridge, he later played football for Aberdeen, and after finishing joined the Police.

There was A Section, B Section and C Section at Grantown School, and I was in C2 Section because back at Cromdale Public School when they'd held the 11 plus exams, I'd been very sick with measles. I fell behind, so even though I still went to the grammar school, I went into the lower group. It had its pluses though because I enjoyed metalwork and woodwork, which I did for three years, as well as technical drawing on a Friday afternoon. The man who took us for these three subjects was Mr Fraser, who was involved with the Army Cadets, and I got on very well with him. I learnt how to make a lot of things – pokers, trowels for digging the garden and a big ironing board for my mother that she used for years. People didn't think we'd amount to much, being in the lower section. I think it was presumed that I would be a labourer-type bloke for the rest of my life, but when I joined the Royal Marines, that changed everything.

My pal Barney Campbell and his older brother Billy followed family expectations after school finished and they had three farms that were amalgamated – East Port, West Port and Upper Port. It was deemed automatically that they'd go and work there, which they did, and they're still there to this day, semi-retired. I'd enjoyed growing up on the farm myself in East Lethendry, but in 1957 the estate factor came round and put the rent up.

One afternoon, I came home from school to find a large family gathering in the kitchen, discussing the fact that earlier in the day a contingent had been out from the estate office in Grantown and increased the yearly rent. It was raised to such an extent that it wasn't economically viable anymore, so our farm and the farm next door were amalgamated. Mr McConachie took them on, and we moved to a smaller farmhouse, five miles down the River Spey, East Achvochkie, Advie.

I had a very happy childhood, but at some point, I became more and more conscious of the fact that I didn't have a father. It had never been a problem growing up on the farm as there were always loads of things to do but being illegitimate did start to weigh on me, and there would come a time when I started to look into who my father was. It was a long way down the line, but piece by piece, from talking to people and using AncestryDNA, I started to find out more about him. I have no recollection of anybody at school asking who my father was, but being in the post-war era, I wasn't alone in that regard. Granny Bell, Margie McLean, Jimmy McLean (Snr), and their sons, Jimmy and Willie, as well as Pat Bell, were good friends of mine and lived nearby. I didn't know anything about Pat's parents and she and I never discussed it. Granny Bell and the McLeans were bringing her up. There were at least two other girls I can think of in the village with no father about, but these things were never questioned.

There were boys and girls I went to school with whose fathers were Newfoundlanders. When all the fit, local men in the area were abroad in the forces during the war, the government recruited Newfoundlanders to cut down the timber in the massive forest on the hillside above East Lethendry Farm. A sawmill was constructed and a lumber camp with huts and dining areas. They recruited a crew of men from Southern Ireland, as well as those from Newfoundland, and one of the Irishmen, it transpired later in life, was my father – James McNabb. I never heard this name from my mother until I was filling in forms to join the Royal Marines because no one in the family ever wanted to tell me much about anything on that subject. It's just how they were, it was the mind-set they had. As far as the older generation were concerned, a lot went on and babies were born, but they didn't think anyone needed to know the real story. I was frequently told, 'The best thing you can do is to let sleeping dogs lie.'

Luckily, Jimmy McLean knew a lot about the Irishmen. He remembered them because he would have been about six years old when they were around. Some of them used to go to Cliff Cottage and play cards and draughts with his father. He was an older boy and a real go-getter kind of guy. As I previously said, I idolised him as a wee loon and followed him around like a little puppy dog for years. He kept ferrets, he set snares and when he was old enough to have a shotgun, I followed him around until he gave me a chance to fire it. Unfortunately, I pushed the safety cap forward at the same time as I pulled the trigger and completely missed the bird that I was aiming for.

A possible scenario would be my mother attending a dance in the village hall, a mile down the road, on the night she first met James McNabb. She was only 19 at the time, and to get back home, she had a lonely country walk ahead of her, in the darkness. My father was amongst the Irishmen from the camp who went to the town to have a few drinks and a dance, and he ended up walking her home. The deed must have been done around that time, but I don't know if she had a lasting relationship with him. Fortunately for me, she got pregnant, and I'm here to tell the tale!

When it was established that my mother was going to have a baby, I think she would have had a hard time. She possibly did not leave the farm and go to the village or into Grantown when she was pregnant, for fear of being judged. As I was growing up, lots of people referred to my uncles Sandy and Peter and Donny as my brothers – I think they just thought I was a latecomer. But it wasn't something I ever placed any importance on at first. Funnily enough, an old bloke called Jock Allanach used to work on a neighbouring farm and occasionally when I would meet him on the road, he'd say, 'Aye, Paddy, how are you?' So he knew my father was an Irishman.

It turns out that I could have met my father, as he died in 1974 when I was a detective sergeant in the Hertfordshire Police.

One of my best mates is an Irishman who helped me initially in my quest, fellow ex-detective Brendon O'Connor, from the Wicklow area. I've always got on very well with the Irish, and he was one of them. I think I took to them and they took to me because it was in the genes – and I've always loved Irish music! Encouraged by my daughter, Dawn, I tried to find out what I could about James McNabb, and at the age of 76, I sent for an AncestryDNA test kit. After a bit of digging and correspondence with key people in my search, the results came back with a 99% match between myself and Jimmy McNabb, who it turned out is my half-brother. Sadly, I found out that my father had passed away, but I learnt that he was born on the 20th of February 1909 in Wicklow, Ireland, and that he had worked at the Irishmen's camp, at the sawmill in Cromdale. After tracing my father's family tree, I also found out about my oldest known paternal relative, Captain Hugh Cameron. He was born around 1700 and was killed at the Battle of Culloden, when the Scottish clans, led by the famous Bonnie Prince Charlie, fought against the English!

In 1958, I left school and started work, because initially, Granny McQueen would not allow my mother to sign the consent forms for me to join the Royal Marines as a junior bugler drummer, which as it turns out was a blessing in disguise. I'd been working in a sawmill and I was getting five pounds a week, which was big money back then, but there was a massive snowstorm for weeks on end and we were laid off because we couldn't work due to the weather, I had to go to the dole office in Grantown to be paid 15/- a week.

By January 1959, I'd worn my grandmother down and she allowed my mother to sign the forms of application to join the Royal Marines' new junior entry scheme, designed to produce future non-commissioned officers for the corps. There was a space for 'Father', so I said, 'What do we put in there?'

My mum just said, 'James McNabb.' Nothing more, nothing less.

Unbeknownst to me, I was going to be in the third intake in this scheme; I couldn't wait to get started! In all honesty, joining the Royal Marines was one of the best things I ever did. I learned to play the Bagpipes, became a Physical Training Instructor, and developed many qualities that I put to good use in a 30-year Police career, retiring with the rank of Detective Inspector. It was partly thanks to them that later on in my life, I went from being just a wee loon to being affectionately known as the 'Tartan Tornado' in the Royal Marines, but that's another chapter.

James McQueen, 4 years old. The Wee Cromdale Loon

At Nethy Games, Myself, my mother Anna, my cousins Helen and Billy Miller,
Mother Margaret, and father Jimmy Miller.

The cairn on Cromdale Hill. June and I caught the hares on the way up. He didn't shoot them.

Cromdale School, primary 6: Helen Miller, Janes McQueen, Barnett Campbell, Gordon Davidson, and Margaret Baxter

Like father like son. James McNabb and James McQueen

2. THE ROYAL MARINES

I first became interested in joining the Royal Marines when I was at Grantown School. I was probably about 14 at the time, and a classmate, Patrick Buchanan, brought in a booklet all about them, with some very smart-looking men on the front cover which I kept on my bedside table and was forever reading through, visualising what it would be like be one of them.

The Royal Marines were like sea soldiers and they travelled all over the world, going to faraway places such as Antarctica, the, Mediterranean the Far East, Arden in Yemen, and Australia. They appealed to me because I'd be on land and at sea and not just one or the other like the Army or the Navy.

On the day I went to join up, I got a train from the Highland Line station in Grantown-on-Spey and went through to Inverness, to the recruiting office, and there I met a chief petty officer from the Royal Navy, who said eagerly, 'You know, it's very difficult to get into the Royal Marines. If you're not successful, would you consider joining the Royal Navy?' Quick as a flash, I answered, 'No, no. If I can't get in, I'll try and get into the Paras.'

There were quite a few other young lads about the same age as myself, probably about eight or 10 of them, and, judging by their accents, they were all local to Inverness. One of them was very loud, and he was going to be on submarines. (I met him a few years later on the HMS Ark Royal, and he was an officer's flunky! I was a Commando leaping out of helicopters.) I remember sitting there completing the exams, and I got through them without any trouble. I had an interview with the chief petty officer, and then that was it, I went back home. The next thing I knew, I got the letter I'd been waiting for, asking me to go down to Glasgow and to be prepared that, should I pass the medical, I would be going to a base in Kent, about 700 miles away. When the time came, my uncle Bill Stevenson, who was married to my Aunty Margaret, was very supportive of me and very encouraging, which I was grateful for, especially as he was ex-forces himself. He'd been in the Army and had also been a glider pilot during the war.

On Saturday the 2nd of May 1959, I got on the train to Glasgow with my little brown suitcase and off I went. My uncle's brother, 'Big' Jim Stevenson, was waiting for me – I'd met him previously in Grantown – and he took the time to show me around. On Monday, he dropped me off at the recruiting office, where I had to complete my medical examination. I remember one of the guys in charge saying, 'You know, your medical is far stricter than for the lads going into the Navy.' There were two other lads with me, one from Glasgow and the other from near Edinburgh, and happily, all three of us were successful in getting through.

The next order of business was to find the NAAFI – a big forces recreational club – and, luckily, it wasn't far away. We were to have our evening meal there before making our way to

Glasgow Central station. There were about a dozen of us, the other recruits being adults, and a big marine sergeant made it very clear that we'd better behave ourselves on the train to London or there'd be big trouble. 'The guard on the train knows all about you,' he said. 'Any problems, and you'll be for it!' The train was a really exciting experience, and although I didn't get any sleep that night, I didn't care. There were all these factories and big cities lit up in a neon glow, and I remember feeling like my adult life was truly about to begin.

Eventually, we got to Euston station, where we were joined by recruits from other places, and all the recruits were assembled together; about 20 or 30 of us, before we jumped on the Tube to travel to Charing Cross. Another new experience for me! From there we made our way to Deal in Kent, and we were formed into three lines by none other than a Scottish corporal of the Royal Marines – Corporal Thompson. I'll always remember, one of the first things he said to us was, 'You're in the Royal Marines now, and not the Army, so don't you ever forget it!'

He got us to march along different streets, and then eventually we came to the big, black barrack gates, where we were met with all the noise and hustle and bustle of our new life. There were lots of Royal Marines in their full blue uniforms with white cross straps, and all the squads were forming up in the large parade ground at 14.00hrs, all at different stages of training. The instructors were shouting and roaring at them, and I thought to myself, 'Well, I've signed on for nine years. It's do or die – here we go!' I spent a year at the Depot in Deal, learning personal hygiene, cleaning kit and weapons, parade ground foot, and rifle drill. Constant periods of physical exercising in the gymnasium, with a lot of importance put on the art of rope climbing. On a Friday afternoon, we would attend a pay parade, salute the Officer, and be given £1.

It wasn't long before one of the instructors pointed out the need to further my education. 'Listen, if you want to get promoted in this role, you've got to get your qualifications.' I had an interview with the officer in charge of Junior Wing Training, Lieutenant Wilson, asking me all sorts of questions in his posh officer's voice, one question being, 'Do you have any hobbies?' I explained growing up on a farm was one long hobby, and I started to tell him about Jimmy McLean and what he and I did. He stopped me abruptly, 'Wait there.' He went out of the room, returned with several instructors, and told me to start again. 'When your squad starts field training we will get you to instruct them how to live off the land like that, excellent skills to have!'

They sent me and the squad, now totalling 30 of us young lads, to school three days a week for 'further education'. That was when the penny dropped for me, and by the end of the year I was qualified educationally to the highest non-commissioned officer's rank – Regimental Sergeant Major. The wee loon from Cromdale was on track. By the end of that year, I was studying not only Maths and English but military typography. Not just how to read a map to get from point A to point B but to fully understand the terrain – streets, woods, valleys – so if you were in pitch darkness at night, setting up an ambush, you would know exactly where you were, every step of the way.

After our initial training at Deal, Kent, we passed out and were now in 'man's Service' and our pay went up to £6 10/- a week. We went to Portsmouth onto the last British Battleship, HMS Vanguard, for two weeks of seamanship training, including gunnery, knots, and splicing broken ropes. Then it was on to Poole in Dorset, where we did two weeks of Landing Craft training, learning how to handle them, and spent two weeks with the Special Boats Service, learning how to paddle large canoes, make explosives and blow things up. Next, we went to Lympstone, Devon, for eight weeks of infantry training, and two weeks of cliff climbing training in Sennen Cove, Cornwall, before going back to Lympstone for the six weeks of Commando training (Full kit and rifle on all tasks, speed marches of four, six and nine miles. Scramble course, Battle P.T. course, 200 yds Fireman's lift, Tarzan course 50 feet up in the trees and Death slide), culminating with the famous '30 miler' across Dartmoor. Having passed, the next day on parade I was presented with my coveted 'Green Beret', before being posted to 41 Independent Commando, Bickleigh, Devon, in October 1960. I remained there until June 1961, when I was drafted to HMS Ark Royal. a former flagship of the Royal Navy.

Letters were sent back and forth between my family and me whilst I was on board the ship, and my Aunty Margaret used to religiously send me the Sunday Post. One of the guys on board the mess deck, a Cockney lad, was always taking the piss out of us Jocks, but more often than not, he'd come up and quietly ask if he could read it too. The post was brought to us in these propeller planes, with all of our letters and newspapers stashed in the belly of the aircraft, in a sort of balloon under the fuselage. I got letters from my mum and from Margaret McDonald, a girl from a neighbouring farm who was in the same class as me in Grantown. When I was training at Lympstone, after completing a rigorous scramble course, I came in from the firing range, covered in muck, had a shower, and then lay on my bed, waiting excitedly for the mail. They used to get somebody from the office to drop it on your bed, and I loved getting letters from Margaret. She'd give me all the gossip – who was doing what and with whom – and I couldn't stop smiling and laughing to myself. On the opposite bed was a bloke called Dave. 'You got something really exciting today, didn't you?' he'd say. 'What are you on about?' I grinned.

In June 1961 I was drafted to Eastney Barracks, Portsmouth, as a member of the Royal Marine Commando Detachment, which was 30 strong, and where most of the others had a lot more service than me. One of the duties we would have to perform was a 'Fisting Party' with four Marines and a Corporal in charge who would have to perform some law and order on a matelot(s)

We joined HMS Ark Royal (crew 2,500, only 30 Royal Marine Commandos) on the actual afternoon of Saturday 5th August 1961, the first day onboard, and were in our Mess Deck (living quarters) storing our kit away, when a big built Chief Petty Officer came in through the door, and shouted, "I need a Royal Marine fisting party". One of our Corporals detailed four of us. I was right behind the CPO as he led us along various passages and down decks until we stopped at a ladder (stairway) down to a mess deck. The CPO told us a matelot was drunk and wanted to fight everybody. I was first down the ladder and he was there, sitting at a table, smoking a fag, drinking from a can, and blood all over him. As soon as he saw us he bellowed obscenities at us in a strong Glaswegian accent. My mate, Ted Kelland, a big Welshman overtook me, picked the table up, and threw it at the bulkhead (wall) as he did, roared at the jolly jack to get on his feet, or words to that effect, whereupon the guy fell to the floor screaming abuse at us. We took him under control with a few punches and carried him to the Quarterdeck. The Officer of the Watch ordered he be placed in the cells. The wee loon from Cromdale had now been involved in a bit of action!!

We went to a lot of different places in the Royal Marines, including Malta, I wasn't old enough to draw a ration of rum when I joined the ship – you had to be 20 – but when the rations were being given out, I'd ask for a sip of the older guys' tot. You'd get sippers, gulpers, and sandy bottoms, depending on how much you drank. A sandy bottom was finishing off the whole lot, with a whole tot being as much as you could have. I wasn't really that into rum, so it was good that we were all allowed two small tins of beer.

When we were on embarkation leave, I took half a bottle of Haig's whisky on board the ship and hid it in my locker. Then I had a particularly memorable New Year after the clock struck 12!

Two Scots lads, Alex Denver and Derek McNeil joined me and we sat around on deckchairs, on the big gun deck, in Grand Harbour, Malta, and after lights out and 12 o'clock came, we drank all of my secret whisky, which I'd had stashed in my locker since August.

Another time, we were off the ship at a training camp in the north of Malta and we were on the assault course when one of the sergeants fell off and broke his arm. It might not have been the most civilised reaction, but we all shared a wicked sense of humour back then, so we all cheered! I met his sister in a pub in Stevenage years later and she told me that this particular sergeant was now working as a civil servant, to which I replied, 'You can tell him from McQueen, that he may be a servant, but he'll never be civil!'

While in the Mediterranean, one evening I heard bagpipes being played, and I located the piper, who when he stopped asked me if I liked the pipes, and I said that I actually did. He went on to say he and others on board were going to form a pipe band, and would I be interested in learning. Being a Scotsman out of Scotland, I assured him I would. So the wee loon from Cromdale was now going to be a 'Piper' that would eventually lead to 39 years of piping stories yet to come.

As well as our time in Malta, we also visited Mombasa in Kenya, which was a very new experience for me. I got roped into a game of football on one occasion between the HMS Ark Royal First 11 and the Mombasa side. They won in the end, 4–1, but that was fine by me. I hadn't even intended to get involved, but the backup engineers and mechanics weren't around that day and a petty officer had come up to the mess deck looking for a few players. My mate, McNeil from Edinburgh, said, 'I'll play, and McQueen here will play for you!' So I was volunteered, but we had fun. It was the first time I'd ever played in front of a crowd, and I said to McNeil when we were having a kick about before the start of the match, 'If you get an orange at half-time, what are you going to do with it?

'Eat it, of course!' he said. 'Why? What are you going to do with yours?'

'I'm going to go behind the goal and give it to one of the little kids as an act of friendship. I don't want to upset these people. I want them to be our friends.' And I did just that.

I was a coxswain (driver) of the Royal Marines liberty boat that was about 30 or 40 feet long and when we were in Mombasa, Old Timber Wood was in charge of the stern and he'd get off and tie the boat up when we got to a jetty. The bowman was a Ginger Wilson and he'd use a boat hook to hook onto something until he could jump off and tie a rope onto a bollard. Our ship, HMS Ark Royal, was anchored in the mouth of the river, and one evening, as it so happened, there was a posh officers' cocktail party going on up on the flight deck, with a whole load of civilian guests from Mombasa, as well as local dignitaries. All these young women in fancy cocktail dresses were going up the ladder on the side of the ship so they could get up onto the quarter-deck, and I was shouting at my mate who was on the bow, 'Wilson, look ahead, not up!' Naughty boy! Years later I met one of the dignitaries when I was having a chat with him in a pub in Stevenage, over a pint of beer after work, Detective Chief Inspector Bob Collingwood.

I always liked a chance to meet the local people, and when we were in Singapore, when I was learning to play the bagpipes on the Ark Royal, I got invited to a local man's house to meet his family. He invited me to his home in a small village in the jungle and I met his wife and his young children, who were all really friendly. I was on the mess deck and he was labouring alongside the engineers, technicians, and tradesmen who were fixing the large gun outside our mess deck. With not much of a common language between us, he was pointing at my bagpipes and saying, 'Pig, pig?'

'No, no!' I replied. 'Moo!' The man thought the actual bag was made from pig skin, and we had a bit of a laugh.

I had to take my shoes off when I arrived at his home, and it was only a wee place, with a little bed and two curious children who came out to greet me. He sent his oldest child to get a boy from further down in the huts who spoke a little English to come up and translate for us, and I got out my maps to show them all where Scotland was. His wife got a tin bath out from under the bed, laid some nice crockery on it and I had something to eat with them all.

We were in and out of Singapore on an aircraft carrier. We'd go for six weeks, come back and then go out for another six weeks, until we changed course and ended up in Manila and Subic Bay in the Philippines.

When in Subic Bay we had a strict warning to only go ashore in groups of four and stick together religiously. They'd say, 'No mucking about, and don't get too drunk!' So we went ashore, behaving ourselves in the bar, and there were all these 'lady boys' coming on strong. Ginger Wilson went to the toilets, and all of a sudden I heard one hell of a noise coming from the cubicle. Bang, crash!! We went in there and he was not in a good way, he was wrecking the place, so we had to call a taxi to take him back to the ship as quickly as possible. When they got him into the sickbay, it became apparent that someone had slipped a 'Mickey Finn' in his drink, a type of dangerous drug. Maybe he'd annoyed one of the lady boys; he might have said the wrong thing to one of them – we never found out – but I learnt a lesson that night.

As well as the Far East, we went to Fremantle near Perth in Australia. The first Sunday night there, myself and a lad called Harris from North Wales went off the ship, looking for a drink, although the pubs closed at six o'clock. We were chatting to some girls and they told us that if we came with them to the Catholic service, we could get some drinks afterwards. We were in the middle of all these hymns and prayers and then we heard bells from the ship – ding, ding! It was a bit of an in-joke. Up in the Far East they'd ring the bells and say, 'Unclean, unclean!' if they knew we were in 'naughty' female company. We met up with the girls on other occasions after that, and we had three nights ashore and one night back on board, on duty. We started taking fags off the ship, which you're not supposed to do in bulk, and we'd change into our civvies. We'd do a lot of drinking in their houses and get back on board for 7 a.m., all pretty knackered.

We even appeared on TV whilst we were in Australia, in our new pipe band kit, which we wore when I was playing the bagpipes on the Ark Royal. We were invited to the television studios in Perth, which was a huge highlight of our time there, and I sang a couple of North East of Scotland Bothy Ballads and had a great time.

We came back to Devonport, Plymouth, in November 1962 and we all got drafted to different barracks. We were lined up and were ready to go down the gangway with all our bags, when two matelots (sailors) came along, who used to refer to us as 'bootnecks'.

'How are these bootnecks getting off the ship at half past 10 in the morning,' one of them said, 'when we can't manage to get off until four o'clock in the afternoon?!'

'Well, they are fucking organised,' his mate replied, 'And we aren't!'

Going back to when we finished our infantry training at Lympstone in Devon, some memorable times we had were two weeks prior to commencing our six weeks Commando course. The officer in charge of our squad was an expert in cliff climbing, and he took us to Helston, to Royal Naval Air Station Cudrose, where we learnt how to climb at Sennen Cove. We learnt three-point climbing, two hands and one foot on the cliff face or vice versa, and climbing in threes, (one behind the other – No. 1 climbs up so far, then No 2 climbs up to him, and so on), and by the very last day, we hadn't had even one accident.

On the very last climb of the last day, an instructor approached me. 'OK, McQueen, you're leading this one. It's 150 to 200 feet and the last 20 feet is a chimney" I eventually reached the chimney; it had three sides and was a pretty high climb. Down beneath me the waves were crashing in, so I was a wee bit frightened, but failure wasn't an option, 'Help mummy, these bad instructors are cruel to me.'

A rope was tied to me and to my number two, so if I fell, I would fall to his level and then the length of my rope past him before I would stop. I got into the swing of things, by pushing my back against one wall and my feet against the other and moving a foot or a hand. An instructor at the top was encouraging me – they were all really good lads.

I have lots of other memories. As we started our commando training, we had to complete the scramble course on Woodbury Common, four miles from the Lympstone Commando Training Centre. I remember my mate, Ginger Hinks, stumbled and was nearly put out of action going around the course, but he got through it somehow, and then we had to double back to barracks and fire off X number of rounds on the 25-yard range. There was a fire bucket near the admin blocks with all this horrible, filthy water, and you'd be so thirsty you'd want to drink it. Then Ginger Hinks, with his bad ankle, had to go to the sickbay. He'd actually cracked the bone, but not wanting to give in he'd gone round the whole course, no doubt in agony.

The commando course was not for the faint-hearted. The morning of the last day we were up bright and early and had a big greasy breakfast in the galley before we went in trucks to somewhere on Dartmoor.

We had to go 10 miles across Dartmoor as a squad with instructors, then 20 miles on the road using our own willpower within a stipulated time of eight hours, wearing full fighting kit and carrying a rifle. I was alongside Barry Saxton as we were going across the moorland, a good lad I'd been with since Juniors at Deal, and I was aware that he was struggling, so I was urging him on: 'Come on, Barry, you can do it, keep going!' When we got to the road, he was still lagging behind, so regretfully, I had to say, 'Barry, I've got to go, mate.' The next time I saw him was the following Saturday morning when we had to go out on parade and get our green berets to show that we were qualified Royal Marine Commandos. We were marching back as a squad when I saw Barry standing with a doleful look on his face, standing by the company office in his blue beret with others who failed. He hadn't made it through, and it was a really sad sight to see. He had to do the whole course again, but fortunately, he passed it.

In the end, it was a medical problem that led to me having to leave the Royal Marines and I was completely gutted. It put me in a bad mood for a while and I even fleetingly considered joining the French Foreign Legion, before I got my head straight. It all started when I was drafted from HMS Ark Royal to Lympstone where I had been selected to commence a three-month Junior Command Course, and I was taking out night patrols. We had to set up ambushes, which we did in the darkness up on Dartmoor, and I had to study a map – where the military topography came in handy. I told the young recruits, 'You've got to be switched on! It might seem like play-acting, but you could be in a similar situation for real, one day.' We set out on the night-time patrol, but then I noticed that my ear had started hissing, and it was really annoying me because I wanted dead quiet. Nevertheless, we did the ambush – shot some and captured others (not for real). Having completed our Junior Command Course we were formed up on parade to be told of our passes or failures, as the case might be. After a three-month intensive course, I qualified to take groups of men for firearms training, parade-ground drill, and physical training. A-passes were promoted immediately, Bs a bit later on, Cs might be promoted at some point, and with Ds they thought there might be some mileage in you yet, so you could try again. Needless to say, E-passes were thanks but no thanks.

They called out five A-passes and I was one of them. 'Go to the clothing store immediately and get your stripes sewn on,' they said. 'Then come back and go to the company office. Corporal McQueen . . . you'll be going on a Platoon Weapons Instructor's course, starting a week on Monday.' Unfortunately, as fate would have it, I ended up having to go to the sick bay that Monday morning as my ear wasn't so good, still hissing.

'What's the problem?' said the chief petty officer. I kind of knew him from around the camp.

I said, 'I've got something wrong with my ear, it's hissing.'

'Right, we'll put some olive oil in it, and cotton wool,' he said, 'then come back down tomorrow and we'll try and syringe it.' The next morning I returned and the Medical Officer syringed out my ear. Afterwards, he said, 'OK, that's you then.'

But the next day it was no different. Before the Monday I was due to start the course, I had to go to Plymouth, to the Royal Naval Hospital there.

'What's the matter with you then, son?' said an Aberdonian medic. 'Just go in that booth there and put those headphones on. When you hear a ping or a pong, press the button on the joystick.'

It turned out that my right lug was well above average, the line from the reading was straight, but the left was like a drunken spider on a piece of blotting paper. I was to immediately have no involvement with the live firing of any weapons for six months and to come back and see them again then.

I was taken off the Platoon Weapons Instructor's course and seconded as a Corporal on the Unit Police. (Called the Provost Staff)

Sadly, after six months it was still the same, so I had to go up in front of a board. There were three medical officers, and they told me that I had suffered damage to my left eardrum which is called traumatic perceptive deafness, as the test shows you can still hear, but not to the standard required for operational duties, meaning you only stay in the Royal Marines as a clerk or a chef, non-combatants or you can take a medical discharge. I took the discharge route and went back out into the wide world, at the age of 21.

When I left the Royal Marines, I went back home for a while and spent some time with my girlfriend, Moira, who was later to become my wife. I had first met her at a dance in Grantown on my last night of embarkation leave prior to going on HMS Ark Royal. I hadn't forgotten her, and when I came back from the Ark Royal I saw her again in the same dance hall and asked her up for a dance. I don't know if Moira was attracted to my fancy clothes – probably just my bullshit, as I was very confident – but after the dance, we started dating. I used to go to a naval tailor called Billy Bernard's, where you could get nice civilian clothes to go out in, and I paid him five bob every week for nearly two years – a lot of money back then. I'd already bought a lovely green, made-to-measure suit in Hong Kong, with a red lining, but I thought I'd get another one from Bernard's. I got properly kitted out there, with shirts and ties and a nice overcoat too.

One afternoon I got all smartened up, ready to go and see Moira, and as I was waiting for the bus from Elgin to Grantown a big Land Rover pulled up next to me. 'Hello there, you look very smart, are you going to Grantown?' said a rather large, posh-speaking chap. We started chatting.

'Yes, I'm going to Grantown. I've just finished in the Royal Marines and I'm on discharge leave.' I told him I was in the Royal Marines for about five years and that I went abroad on the HMS Ark Royal.

'I was in the fleet of arms during the war,' he said, 'as a pilot. What are you going to do with yourself?' he asked.

'I don't know,' I said, 'I haven't really given it a lot of thought.'

'I'm the manager of the distillery here,' he said. 'What's your name by the way?'

'Jimmie McQueen,' I replied knowing Peter McQueen, my uncle, worked for him.

'Well,' he offered, 'I could do with a good man to learn the boiler room and other major areas like the mashing and the still house, and actually distilling the whisky. How about it?'

So I took him up on his offer and had the interview in a moving vehicle. How good was that? I started working for Duncan Grant McGregor, ex-pilot and now manager of the Tormore Distillery, Advie, Morayshire – distilling Long John Scots whisky.

It was hard work at times in the distillery and there was an awful lot of whisky about. The stills could produce about 100 gallons of whisky in one shift – usually the night shift, which then had to be filled into the casks and transported to the large warehouses, then stacked on racks for several years to mature. When they opened the casks after they'd been sent away, they would all come back empty to the distillery, having previously held the finest whisky, which had been matured for X number of years. I never did it, but on the night shift, some of the other men would go out to where the casks were stacked and shake them to see if they could hear any liquid splashing about inside. (This was known as bullin) then have a wee dram for themselves. Probably a sacking offense if caught.

Dry barley would go through a crusher and then get fed into a great big mash tank, like a huge pot, where it would all get mashed up until it was settled. After a period of time, the liquid, called 'worts', was drained off and fed into massive containers, like huge, deep, round, steel tanks, and raw yeast was added so that it could ferment. You'd take the hydrometer readings, and then eventually it was ready to drink. The men called this 'porridge'. Joe and some of them even got hooked on it. They'd rather have drunk that than the whisky.

I worked there for about six months. Having been in the Royal Marines, it didn't seem like a job I should be doing for life, and as I was still young, I knew that there were many more adventures yet to come.

Standing: Genders, McQueen, Hicks. Kneeling: Carson & Dean

Junior Marine McQueen, in full fighting order

The mighty Ark entering harbour.

The young Malayan dockyard worker who invited me to his home

Going on my first exercise as a fighting Royal Marines Commando

The pipe band's first parade on the flight deck April 1962. Marine McQueen in the centre

The Tartan Tornado! I was called this by my Commando oppo's (mates) and Naval Airmen on the Flight Deck

Final two weeks of training to smarten up before being drafted to various ships and Commando Units.

3. LIFE IN THE POLICE FORCE

Moira and I got engaged in Aberdeen, and then, soon after, I joined the police force. In those days, if you were in the police and you got married, they gave you a three-bedroom house. It was unbelievable! I put in a report saying that we were intending to marry on the second of April 1966, and that was it! The next general order came out: PC McQueen, 31 Abbots Avenue West, St Albans. I'd been talking to a guy in a furniture shop in Stevenage and he sorted us out with a nice three-piece suite from an exhibition in London and another for the bedroom, as well as a big double bed. We had no dining room furniture at first and we even had to put the wardrobe by the bedroom window to give us some privacy until the curtains were sorted, but we built things up from there.

In time, Moira got pregnant and gave birth to our son, Gary, in 1968. She was taken to the hospital in the middle of the night, and I had to sit outside, as in those days men weren't present at the birth. It got to 11 a.m. and a nurse came through with the baby so I could see him through the glass. I was on a detective constables' course in Walton Street in Chelsea at the time and completing an intensive three-month course in criminal law, which I finished with an 85% pass. Not bad for a wee loon from Cromdale!

That October we moved from St Albans to the house I live in now, in Stevenage. Our daughter, Dawn, was born in 1971. Gary went into the Army, although he's currently working in security, and Dawn joined the police force, like her dad. She came out recently and has retrained as a sports massage therapist.

I joined the police after I finished working in the distillery, as Moira, who was still my girlfriend then, had spotted an advert in the Press & Journal. Earlier in life, I never had any inclination to join the police, but the time had come to have a rethink.! There was a police force up from Hertfordshire who were recruiting, so I got myself smartened up in my Royal Marine commando blazer, put on my white shirt and my Royal Marine tie and off I went, one Saturday in late 1964, to the Gordon Arms Hotel, Inverurie. The superintendent in charge of the recruiting team who interviewed me was called Bob Oliver, an Edinburgh man, and I think he was impressed. A few weeks later I took an exam at the police station in Elgin, but although I passed they told me that I wasn't going to be able to start until April.

I needed to kill some time and keep the money coming in, so I got in my van and drove up to the west coast of Scotland, to Fort William, and got a job on the concrete squad, building a big pump mill. I was the only man under Black Bob, the man in charge, who hadn't been in prison, but because I was an ex-Royal Marine, I got accepted as one of the boys and I got on with everybody. Most of them were Glasgow 'neds' full of mouth but no action, but then I had a change of heart and decided to go to England to try and get into the police a bit earlier. After New Year in early January 1965, I packed my suitcases and went to the railway station in Grantown-on-Spey, and off I set to Hertfordshire.

As luck would have it, a big train came in and a load of jolly jacks, otherwise known as matelots, were on board from the HMS Ark Royal, all hanging out of the windows. It was 1965 and Churchill had just died, so they were going down to pull his coffin in the gun cartridge. 'McQueen!' some of them were shouting, others shouting 'the Tartan Tornado!' (a name I was known by onboard HMS Ark Royal). Once I was on board, I had the statutory half bottle of whiskey and two of three tins to drink on the way down to Euston, which I shared with some of the matelots in a sort of drinking school.

When I got to Hatfield, I went into the unemployment office and found details of a lady who took in lodgers. I got details of firms looking for employees and secured somewhere to live and a job to start the next morning. Then I went to the police station which was part of the Police Headquarters, but I think they must have thought I was mad. 'Look, they told me I could join in April, but I've come now,' I said. They asked me where I'd stay, so I told them that I'd found a lady who took in lodgers, and I'd got a job in an engineering workshop, starting the next day. Anyhow the bottom line was I had to wait until the 15th of April 1965 to join the police.

Three years doing metalwork under Mr Fraser at Grantown school came in handy when I worked at the engineering workshop —and when it was time to leave, the senior man in the office said, 'You're not leaving, Jimmie, are you?'

'Yeah, I'm joining the police,' I replied.

'Well look, if you don't get on in the police, please come back here. There'll always be a job here for you.'

After three months at the Police Training College, I was let loose on the streets of Hertfordshire.

I was happy when I was a uniformed PC, walking the beat day and night shifts, meeting different people; doing good to some, and arresting others. I formed a bond with another young P.C., Mick Howley, a keen bloke. As time went on I was his Det Sgt. Then further down the line, I was his D.I. and he was my Divisional Commander, Chief Superintendent M.G. Howley. Our bond of friendship would continue when years later I suffered a serious illness.

One morning walking my beat I was stopping cars and checking the driver's documents. I stopped a car and got into the passenger seat. As the driver was fumbling in his pockets I inadvertently pressed the button of the glovebox which sprung open, and inside were a pair of socks, I said, "That's a strange place to keep your socks," and I took them out. As I did I could feel hard things in them and on inspection, I found hidden items of jewellery. He told me he was taking them up to London to sell for a mate! Not believing his explanation I arrested him on suspicion of possessing stolen goods. Later he was charged with burglary. I was given a 'good work minute' on my record of service.

One Saturday afternoon, when I was a PC, I'd been walking my beat in Stevenage town centre, and by the bus station was a café, where there were several youths lolling around the entrance, sitting on the pavement, and people had to step over them to gain entry. One of them, a self-imposed leader, gave me some back-chat in a broad Glaswegian accent, so I took him on verbally. (The Royal Marine in me). I told him if he and his mates were still there when I next came round I'd get a dust truck and personally throw them all into the back of it, and dump the lot of them. That youth was Jimmy Costello, who several weeks later was arrested for an armed robbery, convicted, and sent to Parkhurst prison, on the Isle of Wight, where in an effort to impress London gangland prisoners, he broke a coffee jar, and stuck it into the face of another prisoner, blinding him permanently in one eye. That prisoner was Peter Sutcliffe, the Yorkshire Ripper.

I got a fairly rapid promotion. I was a PC for four years, during which time I passed the Sergeant's exam and attended a three months detective training course. I was a DC for two years. One day my DI came into our office and pinned a notice on the board. He looked at me, confirmed that I had passed my Sergeant's exam, and said I could apply to go on the selection board, for the experience. I wouldn't get through as I was too young in service. I went on the board at Police H.Q. completely relaxed, answering all these hypothetical questions about new policing procedures, crime initiatives and the like. I obviously impressed them because a few months later, I was patrolling Stevenage with three stripes on my arm. In the Hertfordshire Constabulary you always went back into uniform on promotion from the CID. Then six months later I was transferred back onto the CID, on a central detective unit operating from Hatfield. Each D.S had three D.Cs. You'd be doing individual jobs and investigations, but for anything heavy, like an armed robbery, a rape or murder, there would be teams of us that would go out to supplement the local CID.

One day Detective Chief Superintendent Ron Harvey, attended a scene and backed me up when a 17 year old youth who lived near me was trying to murder his father and mother. I had been called over to help by his mother 'battering' my door and screaming at me what their son was doing. He'd poured spirits over them and his father was fighting with him. I ran to the house, the father came out the front door, blood pouring from him, slamming and holding the front door. I went round the back and into the house and took on the youth verbally, who was armed with two knives and as I went towards him he backed off. He went backwards towards the front door, but there was a lot of police activity outside. He eventually started to back up the stairs in front of me. D. C/Supt Harvey (the boss) appeared behind me saying, 'Keep going, James.' When in a bedroom, I got the man to throw down one of the knives. and as he did, I jumped him and we made the arrest. I received a Chief Constable's Commendation.

D. C/Supt Harvey was a great leader and one day he rang me up and said, 'James, my dear friend, the head of the bomb squad wants a good detective sergeant. I've nominated you and you've only got one minute to say yes or no.' I took him up on it and joined the elite Metropolitan Police, Anti-Terrorist Unit (the Bomb Squad), hunting and arresting IRA suspects. I was at a police station in the East End of London, at Limehouse. There was a surveillance unit there where we used plain cars, vans and motorbikes. We also followed lots of targets on foot and recorded everything they did. A detective inspector submitted all the information to Special Branch at New Scotland Yard, so we never really knew what happened with it after that. The best memories I have of the bomb squad are from when I went on the action teams and we used to go out on raids and arrest suspects.

I remember interviewing one particular man whose name was Johnny Hughes. We started the interview and when he was looking at us, I'd never seen such hate from anybody before. I'd dealt with loads of villains by then and had had my fair share of hairy moments, but I'd never experienced any real hatred – only bad words and bad tempers. The hatred in that guy's eyes was something I'll never forget. It was exacerbated a bit because a detective sergeant said to him, 'Ah, Johnny Hughes, bomber – failed.' So, that didn't go down very well.

There were a few memorable cases and characters during my time in the police, and one of the early ones involved Edwin John Fyfield. In the early 70s, when I was a young DC in Stevenage, there were two or three big blocks of flats, just over from the town centre. Complaints were coming in that women were borrowing money and Edwin John Fyfield was working a fiddle and a racket on them. It was a scam that never came to an end. I went over to the flats when he was due to visit and, sure enough, he pulled up in his big, grey Bentley, wearing a big camel hair coat and talking in a very posh voice. I arrested him, and at the police station, interviewed him about the racket and then we had to let him out on bail.

He was due to appear in Stevenage Magistrates' Court on a particular date, but he never did, so we applied for a warrant for his arrest. In the meantime, the fraud escalated, and it was passed to Detective Sergeant Donald Campbell of the fraud squad at police headquarters in Welwyn Garden City. Edwin was circulated as wanted, but lo and behold he then got arrested in Dublin. We applied to get him extradited from there, but to do that we had to fly to Southern Ireland – Detective Inspector O'Reilly, Detective Sergeant Campbell and myself, Detective Constable James McQueen.

On Monday morning, we went to the famous 'Four Courts' in Dublin, the highest court in Southern Ireland, equivalent to the Old Bailey in England, and I was the first one into the witness box giving evidence.

'Detective McQueen, you three officers are not in the Hertfordshire police, you're all members of the Special Branch of the Metropolitan Police,' said the barrister. 'My client instigated a raid on the barracks in Bedford where a lot of rifles were stolen, and that's why you want to get him back to England. It has nothing to do with fraud.'

So, I disputed that. Detective Sergeant Campbell gave his evidence for the offences committed and then it was John O'Reilly's turn.

When we'd arrested Edwin in Stevenage, he spoke with a 'la-di-da, jolly good show, sorry old chap' manner and had been putting on all these airs and graces. But when the barrister asked him to identify himself, he said, 'Yes, I'm Edwin John Fyfield, born in O'Connell Street, Dublin. I have nothing to do with England,' in the strongest Dublin accent I had ever heard. I burst out laughing uncontrollably, so I got a bit of a telling-off for that, from the judge. There he was, this big, posh fraudster, now talking like a man from the backstreets of Dublin. We had to return to England, but we went back again a few weeks later. We never managed to bring him back with us. This was just as the troubles in Northern Ireland were brewing, so by extraditing him to us, to England, I suppose they might have been seen to be going against the wishes of the Irish Republican movement.

Another memorable case came in 1966, and it involved three criminals who were in Shepherd's Bush, London, at the time: Duddy, a Glaswegian; Whitney, a London criminal; and Roberts, an ex-soldier who'd been in Malaya. They were up to something near Wormwood Scrubs, so an anti-crime unit had been sent up there, with a uniformed officer driving and a detective sergeant and detective constable in the back of the car. They saw the criminals and went towards them, intending to talk to them, search them and get IDs, but as the two detectives approached, the criminals got out of their vehicle and shot them in cold blood, in the blink of an eye. They shot the driver and the driver of the criminal's car then ran over one of the detectives, leaving three dead police officers in the dust.

Duddy was eventually caught in Glasgow and Whitney was arrested, but Harry Roberts, being an ex-soldier and having been in the jungle, knew certain skills to survive on the run.

He eventually made his way to a disused airfield near Bishop
Stortford, Hertfordshire, where he set up a camp in the woods.
He was still in contact with his mother in London, who was
bringing supplies out to him whilst he was busy committing
burglaries in the area. A camp of gypsies pulled in somewhere
near this wood and the local PC went up to see what they
were doing. 'You keep getting on to us, but what about that
man in the woods?' they complained.

'What man in the woods?' the PC asked.

'The man camping up there.'

So, the PC found his camp and then discovered that
Roberts had put trip wire all around it, to warn him if
anybody was coming. Fortunately, Roberts wasn't there, so the
PC had a look in the tent and he saw a gun holster, meaning
that Roberts must have the gun on him.

The PC hot-footed it back to Bishop Stopford, and the next
day a large contingent of police arrived, including myself, and
we started searching the area, and the disused bunkers hidden
in thick undergrowth, trying to flush Roberts out. Eventually,
two of the sergeants, rifles in hand, went into this big hay barn
– one of them was Ollie Thorn and the other was Peter Smith,
from Stevenage, who I knew very well. They started moving
hay bales around, and then, there he was, Harry Roberts. He
came out with his hands up and they took him back to Bishop
Stopford. Every pub in the area was full of police officers that
afternoon, drinking pints and celebrating, even though they
weren't really supposed to be out drinking beer. Every time we
dealt with a heavy job or a horrible job, we went down to the
pub and had a good drink. I don't care what anybody says,

that was the finest counselling you could ever have. The local people were out in the streets, cheering and Peter Smith made a TV appearance. It was a very poignant, hectic time.

Another character I remember well was Jetty Loveridge, a gypsy who was causing mayhem in the St Albans area in 1966. He was stealing cars and being an absolute pest, so they formed a group of officers under Detective Inspector Hugh Kirke (a big Irishman), including myself and Mick Howley. We were only young probation constables at the time, so it was unheard of that we should get a place on this unit, but Mick and I already had a pretty good reputation for arresting villains. We were out from 10 p.m. until six in the morning trying to catch Loveridge, without much success, until we got some intelligence that he had a girlfriend in Redbourne Village. We found out where he parked his car at night time to drop his girlfriend off before he headed out on his crime sprees, so we set up an ambush. Mick and I were hiding in a ditch (Commando-style) beside the footpath when we heard his engine and saw his lights flashing, and then it stopped.

'I won't see you tonight or tomorrow,' he said to his girlfriend as they walked past us.

'No, you bloody well won't!' I thought.

We repositioned near his car.

Mick came from behind his Mini as Loveridge was trying to get in, and they started fighting. I came up to the passenger side and tried to get in, but one of Loveridge's tricks was taking the door handles off, so I smashed the window with my truncheon – it went BANG as loud as a gunshot! The other lads told me afterwards that I'd scared the life out of them. I managed to get into the car, grab hold of him round the neck and we'd caught him.

In the mid-70s through to the late 80s, another couple of pests were Robert Brennan and Andy Walsh. Brennan was a big, intimidating Irishman whose nickname was Bob 'The Horse' Brennan. They used to sleep rough in the Stevenage town centre, constantly drinking to excess and aggressively begging for money. One day, they decided to see what they could get from the Roman Catholic Church in Bedwell Crescent, Stevenage, where they threatened Father Reynolds and a young priest called John. Woman Detective Constable Lilly Hillman and I were called to the scene and Brennan and Walsh were immediately arrested. We took statements and asked the priests, should the need arise, if they would be willing to attend court and give evidence, which they did. The next day, Brennan and Walsh had sobered up and were charged with 'demanding money with menaces'. They were told that they would have to go to the magistrates' court and were remanded in custody until then.

In the end, it was decided to send the case to the Crown Court for trial, so when the date arrived the troublesome pair were taken to Luton, where they both entered pleas of 'not guilty'. Our two main witnesses were priests, men of the cloth, so when they went into the witness box and gave their evidence in front of the jury, there was no way any defence barrister was going to challenge their evidence! The jury returned guilty verdicts and both of them were sentenced to five years in prison. The judge turned round to me, took his wig off and said, 'Detective Sergeant McQueen, in all the years

I've been in Crown Court as a Queen's council and as a judge, I've never heard of men of the cloth giving evidence against a defendant!'

I hadn't seen the last of Brennan as it turned out, as one day we got notice that he'd been released and was coming back to town. One Saturday morning W.D.C Lily Hilman was looking out the police station window towards the railway station, when she shouted for me to come and look. I could see Brennan coming towards the police station with a very well-dressed woman. 'Let's go down and have a word with him,' I said to Lily.

'I've just come down to see you, I'm dry,' Brennan said proudly. He was very smartly dressed and the woman with him chimed in, 'I've been visiting him constantly and he's going to come and live with me for a while. He's a changed man.'

'I'm pleased to hear that!' I replied. But the very next morning, he was already back in the cells. This woman had taken him back to her house, he'd raided her drinks cabinet, wrecked the lounge and caused total mayhem until the police came to arrest him.

Sometime later, I was in the detective sergeant's office when a young policewoman came in and handed me a Christmas card from Brennan with a lot of scrawls it. As far as I could make out, it read, 'McQueen, I feckin love you!' He was never far from the cells, and on one occasion I had to let him have a wee glug of the sherry we'd taken off him, just so that his shaking hands were steady enough to sign his statement! He passed away in the cells in Stevenage Police Station from a heart attack, in 1988, and became the first intern in the new cemetery in Stevenage. What a claim to fame . . .

One famous case from Stevenage involved a young 4 yrs. old girl now a woman called Amanda Wright, who has since written a book about it called, Without a Mother's Love. It has also been made into a Sky Crime documentary, Forensics: Catching the Killer. I think of that job every time I pass the house. Amanda's mother, Susan Lowson, had a boyfriend in the house one night. She'd been in bed with him and he'd tried to strangle her and suffocate her with a pillow, because something had gone horribly wrong. He'd murdered her, with four-year-old Amanda in the bed next to her, who he later tried to strangle too. To get rid of the evidence, he set fire to the bed, and then the whole house had gone up in no time. Luckily for Amanda, she had managed to get down the stairs to the front door, a milkman was on his way to work and saw all the smoke, so he kicked the door in and rescued the little girl. Her clothes were on fire, but he managed to get her out and call the fire brigade.

Uniformed officers realised what the score was and cordoned it off as a crime scene, and then CID were called. They found out who Sue was (I knew her father from drinking in the nearby Gamekeeper pub), but we had to find out who the boyfriend was. On the third day of the investigation, the senior officer said, 'We've had a bit of a breakthrough.' DC Peter Harpur, SOCO, found a mug behind the sofa with a fingerprint on it, which identified a man named John Dickenson. D.S Brian Todd had arrested this guy for something else before, so he and DC Jack O'Connor (RIP) went to arrest him. It was a bit of a hectic interview and we still had a lot of work to do to put the case together – you've really got to tighten things up – but we got him in the end and he was sentenced to life. He got parole but was rearrested for historical sexual offences and sentenced to a further 17 years.

Just recently, along with my two ex-colleagues, Brian Todd and Peter Harper, we were interviewed by the Sun newspaper when we met up with Amanda in Stevenage – Jack O'Connor has sadly passed away now. Amanda was quoted as saying, 'If it wasn't for those men caging Dickenson, I would never have found peace. If they hadn't pieced everything together, the man who killed my mum wouldn't be behind bars.'

It was a blessing in disguise leaving the Marines under the circumstances I did, because I'd never have joined the police otherwise.

I was and am proud to say I was a Hertfordshire Police Officer, particularly when I was in Herts CID, held in high regard by neighbouring forces, including the Met. I worked with many top-class men and women and am pleased to say I am still friends with several of them today.

Dawn got her father's number (638) when she joined the Police

Group 1, 'A' Division Herts Police. A fine body of proud men and women

My right-hand man Sgt Ian Carter

DC Dawn McQueen, outstanding Detective work

Detective Inspector Jimmie McQueen. 'A' Division Herts Police

4. PLAYING THE PIPES

O n the Ark Royal one day, I was sitting outside the mess deck one day and I could hear the familiar sound of bagpipes. Initially, I thought it was a cassette, but, wondering where it was coming from, I went and found a Naval Airman playing away, and stood listening until he stopped.

'Do you like the pipes?' he said.

'Yes, I do!' I replied, and he asked if I could play.

'No, no, I can't play, I'm afraid.'

'Well, there's two or three of us on board here, and we're going to get a pipe band up. Do you fancy learning?'

I never gave it a second thought. 'Yeah, I'll learn!'

He was getting a pipe band up, so perhaps subconsciously being a Scotsman I felt obligated to support them.

Not long after leaving Plymouth, long before Singapore, he started teaching me some scales and various movements, and also reading pipe music then, when we got to Singapore, Mr Gibson, the captain of the Ark Royal, directed a lieutenant commander to be in charge of the pipe band. Mr Gibson, who I later found out was very fond of pipe band music and supportive of having one on board his ship, went off to an officer's 'do' with officers from the Queen's Own Highlanders, my local regiment at home, and must have done some sort of a deal with their Commanding Officer.

One day I just happened to be up on the flight deck when I heard a chopper coming. There was this familiar noise as it came towards the ship and landed on the deck and then I saw two soldiers getting out with Glengarry bonnets on, carrying kitbags and pipe boxes. Obviously, the captain had done a deal with the Queen's Own Highlanders C.O. who had seconded two of his best pipers to the ship – Ronald McLean from South Uist and Robert McPhee from Bonar Bridge. They were on board for three months giving us individual tuition on the practice chanter, progressing onto a set of bagpipes, and getting the band together. McLean was even teaching the drummers drumming.

When we got back to Singapore, they went off and two more men came aboard, one named John McDonald from Nairn and Geordie Shanks from Rothes. It turned out that old pipe band uniforms were donated by an RAF band in Singapore and were delivered on board, so when we got down to Perth, we were all dressed up in our own kit. The last night at Subic Bay, we went ashore as a pipe band and we were playing tunes in return for pints of lager. It was drawing in crowds, so we were making a lot of money. People started coming out of the bars, marching behind us all the way back to the ship, because they were all quite inebriated.

The next day, there was an announcement. 'This is your captain speaking. I wish to thank all members of my pipe band for bringing every single member of the crew who was ashore back on board safely.'

If anyone was missing, after we left a port they were usually brought back by the regulating police on other ships. but I remember one of the lads in the pipe band, whose name was Marshall, walking along the jetty in Fremantle, Australia, and shouting to me, 'Bye Jimmie!' He was going ashore with his pipes, but I never saw him again. I don't know what happened to him.

From leaving HMS Ark Royal and the Royal Marines I didn't do a lot of playing, I got them out only occasionally, mainly at New Year.

After I left the police, I decided that I was going to think seriously about playing the bagpipes. I knew I could make money if I got my dexterity up, but I'd never played at a high level by that point. To develop my skills, I went to the College of Piping in Glasgow, also summer schools at the University of Stirling. Later on, I went to London, where I met Jimmy Banks, who had just come out of the Scots Guards 1st Battalion, and his mate Brian McRae, who'd been a Gordon Highlanders Pipe Major and Her Majesty the Queen's personal piper, for 16 years.

I was with these guys for a while, and then I decided to move down to Bristol for work. Brian was a personal assistant to a circuit judge and when he came to Bristol for a trial he said, 'See if you can get me some people together that I can give tuition to.'

I already knew a couple of girl pipers whom I had met at the Stirling Summer Schools – one of them had invited me to a place in Wiltshire where they'd put a pipe band together for an Armistice Day event – and I knew a couple of blokes too. There was a lieutenant commander in the Navy and a Scottish soloist champion piper, so I got a little group together and it grew from there. That was the formation of the City of Bristol Pipes and Drums. We played the pipes for a march, and when we finished we went for a drink at the British Legion Club. On one occasion, Campbell De Berg, the lieutenant Commander, asked me if I was in the Royal Naval Piping Society. 'You should join. We go on marches every February to Cologne in Germany.'

'That sounds all right!' I thought. I did five of these yearly marches.

In the summer of the year 2000, I was home in Cromdale, sitting in the Haugh bar across the road from my old school, and started to form a plan to take my band up to the village. The owner of the bar/hotel agreed to feed us and I arranged with Irene Galasso, for members to sleep in my old school, now an outdoor centre. She said I could use the outdoor centre for a few nights and she really helped to promote us as she worked with the Highland Council. She told everybody about the band, and then we got a load of money from the tourist board too! I was on television and on the radio down in Bristol, being interviewed. We played the Newtonmore Highland games, and prior to leaving on our coach, one of the officials handed me two bottles of Grouse whisky – by the time we got to Grantown, they were both empty. I will tell you about me playing on the piper's stone on Cromdale Hill later.

It's more or less impossible to learn a tune on a set of bagpipes, so you use the practice chanter first and practice until your tutor feels ready to progress onto the pipes. What did make it a bit easier for me was the fact that I knew a lot of Scottish tunes in my head as a result of going to Scottish country dancing. We sang the words to them at school and at home, when there was Scottish dance music on the radio. When the two lads from the Queen's Own Highlanders came on board the ship in Singapore, we learnt 'The Skye Boat Song' and then faster tunes like 'Scotland the Brave'. One of the songs I liked singing was 'Take me Back to the pipe tune, the Meeting o' the Waters.

Something I enjoyed about piping was the fact that you've got to be a bit of a showman, and getting applause was a great feeling, so I decided that perhaps I could play at weddings and funerals to earn a bit of extra money. I got many letters and thank you cards over the years, and through my association with Jimmy Banks up in London, I ended up going to Edinburgh on two separate years, when they had a thousand pipers and drummers marching up Princes Street, which were exhilarating experiences.

Fairy-tale Weddings do come True, a London Company, hired me to play at a wedding on the 17th of August 1996 at the Lochmulardoch Hotel, Invernesshire, 21 miles into the mountains from Loch Ness. During the week I was playing at the Bretton Folk Festivals, in Brittany, North-West, France. They flew me from Brest to Charles de Gaulle Airport, Paris, to Heathrow, and finally to Inverness Airport, where I was taxied to Lochmulardoch. Later I received a thank you letter:-

Jimmie McQueen, Thank you very much for playing the bagpipes so well at our wedding on Saturday the 17th of August 1996. We had a great day and your playing "the pipes" made it even better. For many people as well as us. Thank you once again. Louise and Sean Holton.

Another time, there was a funny incident involving John Carlisle, the MP, who'd been pontificating in the Houses of Parliament, saying that bagpipes should be banned forever. The Scottish Daily Mail reporters had telephoned down to London, to a colleague there, to see if anybody played the pipes, and this colleague knew me. The plot was, if I was up for it, that they would take me to Carlisle's place in Bedfordshire at daybreak, and then I'd strike up a tune on the bagpipes, right outside his house. I was up for it, obviously, because that's the kind of guy I am.

When the time came, I was ushered underneath his bedroom window in my full kit, and I struck up my pipes with gusto! The next thing I knew, there was a lady looking out of the window, Carlisle's wife, but I don't know if she was involved in the plot. She was clapping and cheering like it was the best thing she'd ever seen, and she came down wearing a big Scottish scarf. Eventually, Carlisle appeared, and the next thing we knew, the story was all over the Scottish Sunday Mail. The next time I went home on holiday and saw my pals in the pub, I got a round of applause. 'Oh, here he is! McQueen the piper! Well done, Jimmie!'

After being in the police, I worked for Securicor in London, who had their own magazine, and I sent a photo of myself to the editor and a write-up about my piping, which they published, and I got a phone call from a man called Bill

Trotter, who was based in Istanbul, working for Securicor. He wanted me to go out there to play the pipes.

'We've got a big St Andrew's society here in Istanbul,' he said, 'and we have a lot of functions raising money for ex-pats who've fallen on hard times, who are scratching out a living. We have a Scottish week where we have chefs out from Scotland, the finest sirloin steaks, and the best whiskey – you name it, we've got it! Would you be able to come out for a week?'

In the end, I went out there for 10 days and was booked into the Swiss Hotel, the biggest in Istanbul.

'Look, can you come down to the foyer? We've got some special guests arriving,' the manager said one day, and it was the Kennedys from America. Not John F Kennedy, but members of his family, so I piped them in as they came into the hotel.

That night, I was playing in the foyer and I marched along to where the lifts were, just as the Kennedy party was coming down to dinner. I piped them into the restaurant, and later on, I had a few whiskies with some of them at the bar – they were very friendly and down to earth. There were a few dignitaries coming down to these evening meals, and there'd be glasses of Edinburgh crystal which they'd put on the tables, in front of the guests, along with the finest Scotch whisky.

I must have done a good job as I got invited back the next year as well. All in all, I went out there four times – I loved it. I got to know the waiters and they'd give me the odd half-empty whisky to take back to the room, very nice whisky. Some evenings, maybe a nice lady would come up and say, 'We're having a party when we go back to the house. Would you like to come and join us? We will lay on transport, and bring your bagpipes.' I'd go to these big houses with big wrought iron gates and play the bagpipes whilst they sang and enjoyed themselves.

The trips to Istanbul were all expenses paid, so I was very lucky. It was great. I got to Heathrow Airport on one occasion, and as I was about to start boarding the plane with my pipes – I never put them in the hold – a steward came and asked why I was going to Istanbul. Sometime after we had been flying for a while he came up to me and said that the captain would like me to go up to the cockpit. The co-pilot was flying the plane, and the pilot turned round to me and said, 'We'll shortly be flying over Brussels. Could you perhaps strike up your bagpipes and play up and down the aisles?' So, I set my pipes up, played a bit of a tune for the pilots, and then I went along the aisles, much to the displeasure of those passengers who were asleep!

When I played the pipes at funerals there was always a sense of satisfaction from doing a good job. On one occasion, I piped a hearse down to the crematorium, and the weather was terrible, so an older gentleman took a handkerchief from his pocket and wiped the rain off my face. At another funeral, I piped a coffin down to the grave site and a man held an umbrella above my head to keep the wind off me and my pipes. I always felt that my presence was appreciated.

I went to a natural burial ground once, north of Bristol, down in the woods, and the lady was Scottish and had two sons in kilts. They had to bring the coffin in a hearse, and a carriage and horse were waiting for it, so I started walking alongside the horse. I started talking to him, stroking his neck, and as we set off, I struck up my pipes. The woman driving the carriage was all dressed up to the nines, and as it was a frosty day, I could feel the horse snorting – I could feel his breath on my shoulder. He was pulling the coffin; I was playing the pipes just in front of him, and it was like he wanted to join in. When the woman got down from the carriage she said, 'He wanted to be with you, Jimmie! I had to keep holding him back!'

As far as weddings were concerned, I quickly cottoned on to the fact that I could get a lot of work from bridal fairs. Many of them were held at big hotels, so I booked a table, set up a stand and got to know the people who organised them. To alert people to the fact that I was there, I used to go and play my pipes for the brides and grooms. I used to sweet talk the woman in charge and she would let me lead out the bride and groom with my pipes, onto the catwalk. I went up to play my pipes on the stage in Bristol once, and in front of the crowd, I said to the wedding celebrant, 'I thought you told me that I'd be playing for people going to a wedding, but this crowd look more like they're at a funeral! Come on people, let's get a bit of life into you!' Then I struck up a tune and they all started clapping. Another piper, in the pub one day, said to me that he was worried about not getting many bookings, so I told him that you have to have a bit of patter, a bit of banter with the crowd.

Back then I'd charge about £150 for a wedding, and I'd charge the same for a Burns Night supper, where organisers would also want someone to address the haggis, they'd ask me, can you do that poem thing? 'Yes, I can for an extra £50!'

'Fair fa' your honest, sonsie face, Great Chieftain o' the Puddin-race! Aboon them a'ye tak your place, Painch, tripe, or thairm: Weel are ye wordy of a grace, As lang's my arm . . . '

There were other verses, but after that, I would stab the haggis, have a salute and then they'd cry, 'The haggis! The haggis!' I'd get people standing up for the last verse and try to get a bit of audience participation.

When I was setting up the pipe band in Bristol, I thought it would be great if we could have a well-known local man as our president, and was delighted when Donald Cameron accepted my proposal.

Donald Cameron is a Scottish balloonist, and founder of Cameron Balloons, Bristol – the world's largest hot air balloon manufacturer. He is one of the few aeronauts to be awarded the Harmon Trophy, as the 'World's Outstanding Aviator'.

Two years in succession he took a group of balloonists from Europe and elsewhere on ten-day trips around Scottish distilleries, and I went along and piped them into the various establishments. Most evenings, prior to dinner, I would pipe in haggis and Donald's friend, Muir Moffat, would take great pride in doing, 'Robbie Burns Address to a Haggis'.

Great tours with lasting happy memories.

Weddings were fairly joyous occasions, but I liked doing the Burns Nights, which were a more raucous type of event. I had my own website and it generated bookings.

Perhaps my proudest moment as a piper was taking the City of Bristol Pipes and Drums to Cromdale in 2001, to play on the Piper's Stone. Folklore says that Hamish, a wounded Jacobite piper, during the Battle of Cromdale in 1690, made it as far as a boulder by two Scots pines, where he stood and piped tune after tune to encourage his comrades until he eventually collapsed. Who would have thought that, 300+ years later, it would be me who stood on the same stone, surrounded by my pipe band, proudly playing 'The Haughs o' Cromdale' to my native villagers, people from the surrounding community, and my family.

Band Practice on HMS Ark Royal

Piping on the 'Pipers Stone'

Playing at a Wedding

Piping at a funeral

WAKE UP YOU CHANTER

Early morning lament for a lamentable MP

I'LL BE BLOWED · EAR WE GO · PIPE DREAM · HUIK AWAKENING

Raw

THE dawn chorus rises into slate-grey skies, cutting like a dirk through the English early-morning chill.

It is 7.30am, and the Bedfordshire county set are awakening for a weekend of huntin', shootin' and fishin'. Somewhere a dog barks.

But hark – that is no bark. Or even a lark.

Sounding across the rolling heartland of middle England is the raw, shrill and unmistakable sound of the BAGPIPES.

And as a curtain twitches, and the head of English MP John Carlisle appears at an upstairs window, a basic truth dawns...

REVENGE IS SWEET.

For the skirl of the pipes may not have stirred Mr Carlisle to tearful emotion, but his comments of a few hours earlier very definitely stirred the blood of Scots everywhere.

The right-wing Tory's remarks during a noisy debate in Parliament this week prompted the *Sunday Mail* to send brave-hearted piper Jimmy McQueen to the MP's large country farmhouse at Henlow in Bedfordshire.

So, yesterday morning, the Tory member for Luton North received a rude awakening after daring to blow derision on the bagpipes.

As Jimmy played him a stirring march, called *The Haughs of Cromdale*, John Carlisle covered his ears. But he was unrepentant.

Love

The 53-year-old MP said: "I love everything about the Scots. I love the people. My wife is a Scot.

"I love fishing and shooting in Scotland. I love the country. I go there frequently. I enjoy whisky. But I cannot stand the bagpipes."

And as Jimmy played on, Mr Carlisle said: "I tolerate everything else except that ghastly machine."

But his wife, Anthea, said: "I'd like to be woken up every morning by the sound of the pipes."

Piper Jimmy, also 53, is an ex-Royal Marine and a member of the City of London Pipes and Drums Band. He's been playing the pipes for 30 years. His chosen march, *The Haughs of Cromdale*, comes from Jimmy's home village near Grantown-on-Spey.

Jimmy said: "The English tried to suppress the pipes in 1745. They weren't successful and John Carlisle won't be now."

Heed

● Mr Carlisle would do well to heed the words of an auld Scots sang from that very same 1745 rebellion, about another Englishman called John – Hey Johnnie Cope Are Ye Waukin' Yet? It gangs:

"I'm now Johnie, got up and die, The highland bagpipes make a din.

"'Tis better to sleep in a hale skin.

"It'll be a bloody mornin'."

● And a line from *A Hundred Pipers* (m'a' an' a'):

"...And we'll on and march them to Carlisle Ha'..."

Early morning call for the naughty MP

Typical Bridal Fayre, plying my trade as a Piper.

Advertising: (01462) 423420 • Editorial: (01462) 420120 • Sport (01727) 846950

Piper takes his music around the world

THE skirl of the bagpipes will soon be heard amongst the minarets and temples of mysterious Istanbul, thanks to former detective Jimmie McQueen.

For Jimmie, who used to be an inspector based in his home town of Stevenage, is flying out to Turkey to play the pipes at a number of trade events being organised to promote Scottish businesses.

His skill with the pipes is well known in North Herts and he has played at countless weddings as well as Burns Night celebrations and other Scottish events.

But now his rousing sounds will be heard for the first time on the border where Europe meets Asia.

Jimmie will fly out on St Andrew's Day on Thursday and stay at the world famous Swiss Hotel in Istanbul.

◆ Jimmie McQueen practises for his trip to Turkey

BY ROSS FRANCIS

The week long event is to promote Scottish business but Securicor, who Jimmie now works for, will also be taking part.

The company hopes to win lucrative contracts providing security for office blocks, banks and cash-in-transit services.

Since leaving the Hertfordshire Force four years ago Jimmie has concentrated on improving his pipe-playing skills. He has studied at the College of Piping in Glasgow as well as the University of Sterling.

Jimmie said: "Such is the demand for Scottish pipers around the world, I would like to see an agency formed that could provide a single piper or a full pipe band for any occasion.

Vandals hit town

A RESIDENT living in Round Mead, Stevenage, had a brick thrown through a window at his home during the early hours of Sunday morning. The matter has been reported to police.

The windscreen on a Ford Sierra belonging to Valerie Powell was smashed while the car was parked in Blenheim Way in the town on Tuesday evening.

The same evening two tyres on a Montego were slashed while it was parked in Ripon Road, Stevenage. The vehicle belongs to Peter Wright.

Piping in Istanbul

First Wedding I played at

Piping course Stirling Uni. 1992

Hogmanay with John and Irene Copeland

5. TUG OF WAR TRIUMPHS

My piping skills were called for during my police career occasionally. For example, one Saturday evening, I was having a drink in the police social club in Stevenage when two PCs came up to me, smiling, and said, 'Jimmie, we're doing basketball tomorrow for Stevenage Day, dressed as tarts. Would you come and pipe us on please?'

'OK . . .' I said, and I went down there next day. Sure enough, they were dressed as tarts, in skirts, with long wigs, stockings, and suspenders. I piped them on and stood watching the competition, then a lad in a rugby shirt and boots came up to me. 'You don't know me,' he said, 'but I'm a PC from Hitchin. My name's Graham Walker. A load of my mates are doing a tug of war. Could you pipe us on?'

So I did, they won, and then they made it to the finals against a team called The White Lions. The prize was a barrel of beer.

There was abuse and catcalling coming from the opposing team, and I recognised several of them as being what we would call CROs – people who have a criminal record. Graham and his team lost the first round, but I started coaching them, still in my kilt and holding my bagpipes until, unfortunately, they lost.

Graham came to me and said, 'The bastards won't give us a fucking drink out of the barrel.'

'That's not very nice,' I replied, but I told him, 'There's a beer tent nearby and I'm going there for a drink, why don't you come?' The man behind the bar was Fred Anderton from the Times Club, near the police station.

'Good afternoon. It doesn't look like you're in a very good mood, Jimmie.'

'No, I'm not,' I said, but I asked him, 'Have you got a family day this year?'

'Yes, in two weeks,' he replied.

'Right. Well, I'll look after the bar and you go and invite that White Lion tug-of-war team to your family's day. Dont mention the word 'Police'.' Fred came back and said they wanted to get involved, so I told him to try and make sure they did.

I went to the police station and found a sergeant who used take lads to tug of war for fun days, and I got the telephone number of a coach, Sid Goss, from the nearby village of Walken, who got involved too and was also sworn to secrecy. On Monday morning I saw D.S Brian Todd and we got several D.Cs together. When we called a briefing, they thought it was about a police raid or something, but we briefed them to take part in the tug of war and explained that a score had to be settled and our modus operandi (M.O.) would be two weeks of training and failure would not be an option. We trained for two weeks, out at Walkern, pulling weights up and down a gantry, then went to the Times Club . . . and we ripped the White Lions team out of the ground, two straight pulls, and won a big barrel of beer! The mayor even came over to congratulate us and presented the trophies. We had some photographs taken and the White Lions team could be seen in the background looking dead sick. It was job done, and that's how I got into tug of war.

Quite a few of the lads said they were never doing it again, but we had an influx of new blood, with me and a few others, and we started pulling on Saturdays in an inter-club competition in Bedfordshire. I stopped taking part after a while, but I began training police teams, who ended up entering the Police Nationals, where we eventually won silver. My general training in the Royal Marines was a distinct advantage, the mindset they instilled in me, and finally, I was a qualified P.T.I.

The policewomen wanted equality, but at that time they were always separate from the blokes and they weren't integrated onto the same shifts at first. Undeterred, they pestered me to form a tug-of-war team and a lot of pubs in the area then started getting women's teams to compete. Little did I know one day some of them would go on to win gold medals in Tokyo! Eventually, the women's teams from the pubs got fed up with being beaten by the police teams, who basically were trained too well by me, and a local reporter picked up on this and did an article in the News of the World about it. A man from Scunthorpe who had read the article got in touch with me by letter saying, 'We've got a lot of good teams up here, why don't you come to some of our competitions?' So, I did, and we started winning up there. At one point, they won the Ladies' Tug of War National Championships.

Myself and the policemen pullers had to register with the English Tug of War Association, but there came a point where one of the rules was that you mustn't be involved with any other associations. They wouldn't accept the ladies into the English Tug of War Association and they were going to ban me from being a member of it, if I was involved in coaching any teams who were not members of the E.T.O.W.A. That would have meant that I couldn't pull or take my team to any competitions or national championships. The man who threatened me was the secretary of the English Tug of War Association, Peter Craft. I told him that I was going to take it to the press, to my local MP, to Parliament, and, if necessary, to the European Court of Human Rights at The Hague because it was discrimination of the highest order. Eventually, he backed down and the women were allowed to be in the English Tug of War Association.

It was a major breakthrough for me and the ladies. Having won the Ladies English Tug of War Association competition, we then went to Scotland and won the British Championships, and then we went to Ireland where we won bronze in the European Championships. We went to Sweden for the invitation competitions and to Holland for the World Championships – an indoor tug of war where you pull on rubber mats. Two of my ladies team got selected to go to Tokyo, where they pulled for the England indoor team and won gold medals.

One of the women was W.D.C Lily Hilman, who had joined the ladies' team when she used to watch the men in the early days. She'd asked me if she could join, but, initially, I'd said no because I thought she was too old. That riled her Irish temper and she expressed her views about my comments quite forcibly. She certainly proved me wrong when she won the gold medal in Tokyo – I also had the pleasure of training my son, Gary, and his pals, pulling indoor tug of war, and they competed at a Youth National Competition, in Gateshead, County Durham, against tough opposition from Army teams, They gave a very good account of themselves, winning bronze medals.

On the 24th of June 1983, I, Detective Sergeant Jimmie McQueen, won top prize, and I was very proud to receive a big, shiny wooden trophy from the Mayor of Stevenage for my services towards reigniting the sport of tug of war in the Stevenage area.

Tug of War English National Champions

Hertfordshire Constabulary Tug of War Squad

Erecting our training Gantry, the concrete barrels for pulling up and down can be seen at the foot of the 30' pole

a heavyweight ladies of Rothwell took some shifting during a ladies' tug-of-war competition staged in Scunthorpe by the Scunthorpe Ladies' Tug-of-War Association. en teams took part in the event, held at the Grange Farm Hobbies Centre, and the hwell team came second in the "catch" competition. [More pictures — Page NINE.]

The Stevenage policewomen went north to Scunthorpe beating seven teams to win against the 'mighty ladies from Rothwell'

*Stevenage Policemen win the inter-divisional tug-of-war competition at
the annual Force Sports Day*

*26th October 1980, Stevenage Police Women have their first pull outside
the Crooked Billet pub, and they won*

Trophies presented by the Mayor. White Lion pullers are in the background.

Detective Sergeant Jimmie McQueen, No 2, drives his team backward winning two successive ends

Woman Detective Constable Lily Hilman, Gold Medallist Tokyo 1988

Hertsmen!! Silver medallists P.A.A. Hendon, London. 1991

At the U.K. Championships on 6th September 1987, Stirling we were supported by my family members from Cromdale

English Ladies Tug of War Association National Champions 1986

D.C. George Corkin pulling my leg! at my promotion 'Do' D.S. to Inspector

7th, July 1980, Stevenage CID Officers train to pull tug-of-war with D.S Jimmie McQueen. Failure is not an option!!

Indoor training for World's Tokyo 1988

Herts Policewomen are powerful pulling at the 'Euro's' 1987

The 'Euro's' 1987

6. MY SPINAL INJURY – LIFE GOES ON

I n February 2009, I was working at Heathrow, at the immigration removal centre as a contract compliance manager, living during the week in a place called Hanwell. In the mornings I used to get in the car and drive to the local David Lloyd fitness centre for 6 a.m., where I'd do an hour's session – either swimming or working on the machines – and then I'd have a shower and shave and get dressed, ready for work. I'd get to work about 7.30 a.m., all fresh and ready for the day ahead.

Everything suddenly changed during the night of the 9th of February.

After waking up and being violently sick, I began one of the greatest trials of my life, fighting an infection that left me in a coma for 12 days. The monitor at Ealing Hospital showed that my heart rate was excessively high, my liver and kidneys weren't looking good and one lung had collapsed, necessitating a tracheotomy procedure.

I had an MRI scan and the medics decided that I would need an operation, which meant a transfer to Charing Cross and a major procedure. When I eventually came out of the coma, I woke up and my daughter, Dawn, was by my side.

'Dad, you're very ill,' she said. 'They've operated on you ... but you're going to be paralysed from the neck down.' It wasn't the best news obviously, but there wasn't a lot I could do about it at first.

After about six weeks, I was transferred to Lister Hospital in Stevenage and I had a lot of visitors. There were quite a few of my ex-colleagues from the police, from the CID in particular, and one of them was my old mate, Mick Howley. Mick being Mick, he took charge, and started talking to the physios. Together with another couple of good colleagues and friends of mine, Brian Wilson and Richard McGregor, both ex-detective sergeants, they organised a course of action.

They used to come into the hospital every morning and work on my hands, my fingers, my arms and my legs. Eventually, they got one thumb moving and my hand moving a little bit, and there were great discussions as to how we were going to move forward and perhaps find extra support away from Lister Hospital. Mick was pressing the management at the Lister and organised me being transferred to Stoke Mandeville, Aylesbury, Bucks, to the National Spinal Injuries Centre there, because my operation had caused so much damage to my spinal cord.

On the day that I was transferred, I was wheeled in and I remember it all vividly. I remember going up in the big lift, up to St Andrew Ward, and then to the side ward, where there was a team of doctors and nurses around me, as well as the top hospital director and the man who was going to be my consultant. Mr. Saif. I was on the ward for about six weeks, and when I was physically capable of sitting in the wheelchair for a minimum of four hours, I was transferred to St George Ward, where my rehabilitation began. I had a team of physiotherapists and had to go to the big gymnasium where they had all different kinds of machines, swings and hoists. Selina Sawah was my physio. There was occupational therapy – Susie Scorer was my physio – and that's where she made me do exercises for my hands and fingers to try and get them going again. I joined a handwriting class and they made a special brace that went over my fingers so I could hold the pen. I had one of my bagpipe music books sent in, which made me happy as I was going through the tunes in my head as I was writing the music down. A gentleman called John took that class, and one day he said, 'Jimmie this is your last session in this class.' I asked him why? He replied, 'You've become too good.'

There was the hydrotherapy and the swimming pool, and the main lady there was Deryn Creasy, a great woman, who'd exercise my arms and legs in the pool, which really helped. In the gymnasium, there was also a bicycle that could be pedaled by hands or feet, called the FES – the Functional Electrical Stimulation bike – which used pads to send electronic pulses to various muscles in the body so when you were pedalling it helped your muscles to operate. That really brought me on a long way.

There were hoists to help me stand and wooden standing frames, and they'd get me up to try and stand for a half hour or so. It was a great place with exceptional professional staff, and I'm so grateful to them as they worked wonders. One year later, in April 2010, I'd regained quite a lot of mobility and I could nearly walk, using a frame, so the consultant, Mr Mofid Saif (MD-FRCS-FRCP), decided it was time for me to be discharged. He used to say to me, 'You are a very determined man, Mr McQueen.'

During my time at Stoke Mandeville I had lots and lots of visitors; my family, various friends, and former CID colleagues, two of whom to this day come to meet me in a pub in Stevenage every six weeks or so. David Walker, former D.S. and Mick Buttle, former Chief Superintendent. All the officers I have mentioned worked at one time or another with me as P.Cs on the beat, showing that deep bond, we Hertfordshire Police Officers have to this day.

Mick Howley was at the forefront of helping me and decided that he'd mastermind the building of an extension on the side of my house. He got various builders, carpenters, electricians, and roofers to put it together, and he'd turn up every morning, with his team, for about three months. They were brilliant.

Once I was back in Stevenage, I was taken under the wing of a physio at Lister Hospital called Wendy Forsyth, who helped me to rejoin the David Lloyd gym in Stevenage. They were quite happy to have me and my wheelchair in the gym, on the proviso that I had a personal trainer, so I found a fine young man, James Bahagiar, and even discovered that he was the grandson of a lady that I'd worked with in the police. He used to make me use a manual wheelchair, which I pushed back and forth to strengthen my muscles.

After sessions with James, I had a hydrotherapist called Ben Ruby, who came with me to the swimming pool at David

Lloyd's. Next, I bought a full-sized tricycle that I keep in my garage. My latest personal trainer, Claire, with the help of my carer Elizabeth, get me onto it, and away we go, round the local park.

I'm lucky really as I still lead an active life and I regularly see my family and friends, as well as having a helping hand from my carers, Elizabeth, Gertrude, and Paula, who have been with me for nine years now. I've got three grandchildren, two boys and a girl – Stuart, Ramsay, and Ella, and three great-grandchildren – Lily-Grace, Oliver and Ethan. We get together whenever we can.

In January 2023 I went up to Grantown-on-Spey to celebrate Burns Night as well as my Uncle Sandy's 90th birthday and my 80th. Seventeen family and friends helped to make it a joyous evening.

There's no real reason why I couldn't walk again, and I was going well towards it until the first big lockdown due to Covid, in March 2020. That scuppered things quite a lot, but I've been able to go back to my exercises in the gym. I'd lost a lot of strength in my legs and my hydrotherapy lady at the swimming pool moved away from Stevenage, but I'm still hoping to get that started again. I'm just going to make the best of a bad job now. I'm getting stronger, the anti-gravity treadmill helps, and my injury is what has been classified as incomplete, which means that the spinal cord is not completely severed. It can still take messages from the brain to my muscles.

I can do a lot more with my right hand and arm now, and my personal trainer uses a little electronic gadget called a functional electronic stimulation device on my biceps, so we're working towards doing more exercises. I go to a hall where there are a lot of badminton courts, and I use my walking frame to practice walking.

A good day to me these days starts by getting up with a sense of purpose. After breakfast, I usually have a bit of a chat with others on the bus travelling to the gym. I like to do a bit of work on my laptop when I get home and I try not to turn the television on until about five o'clock, when I'm happy to watch the football or catch up with the news. I'm definitely not an advocate of sitting around doing nothing.

Getting on and of buses is made easy as there is a ramp provided. Likewise, if you travel by train, they provide special assistance, as they do at airports, to get you on and off planes.

For me, life as a disabled person flying a wheelchair is not too bad. There are a lot of people a lot worse off.

My advice to future generations would be to go for what you want to do in life and then just get stuck in. I got my initial work ethic as a boy at home, working on the farm, and I learnt back then that you don't get something for nothing. In a nutshell, I'd have to say that you need to listen to your gut and then just put in the hours and the hard work. Do your best at everything you do.

To conclude, The next item on my agenda is a trip over to Ireland to see where my father was born, and the house he lived in up until his passing, and then pay my respects at his grave, where I will thank him for giving me life.

Jimmie McQueen.

3rd April 2023.

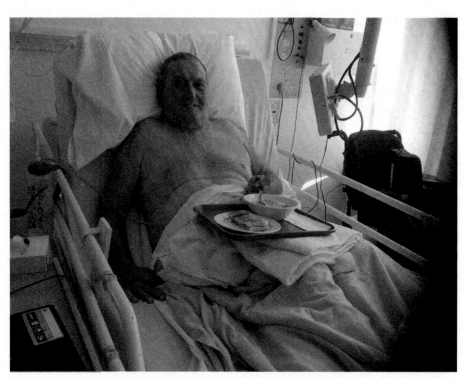

I spent a year in that bed, Stoke Mandeville

Physios trying to get me standing up

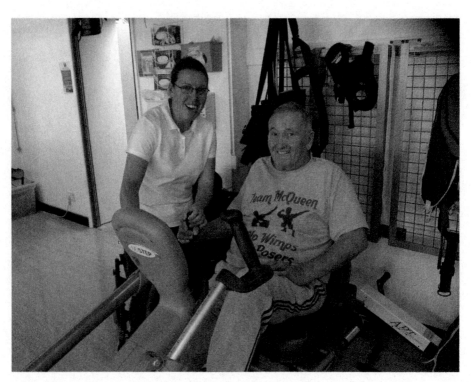

Exercise machine at Stoke Mandeville

Hydrotherapy in the pool with Physio Rachel

Now at home visiting the Bakers shop on my tricycle

With my daughter Dawn and son Gary, meeting my niece Tracey McNabb. Our own flesh and blood from Ireland

Printed in Great Britain
by Amazon

38648299R00076